Amazing Mammals

WRITTEN BY
ALEXANDRA PARSONS

PHOTOGRAPHED BY
JERRY YOUNG

Dorling Kindersley · London

Editor Scott Steedman
Designers Ann Cannings and Margo Beamish-White
Senior art editor Jacquie Gulliver
Editorial director Sue Unstead
Art director Anne-Marie Bulat

Special photography by Jerry Young
Illustrations by Ruth Lindsay and Julie Anderson
Animals supplied by Trevor Smith's Animal World
Editorial consultants
The staff of the Natural History Museum, London

First published in Great Britain in 1990 by
Dorling Kindersley Limited
9 Henrietta Street, London WC2E 8PS

British Library Cataloguing in Publication Data
Parsons, Alexandra
    Amazing mammals
    1. Mammals
    I. Title   II. Series
    599

    ISBN 0-86318-433-2

Colour reproduction by Colourscan, Singapore
Typeset by Windsorgraphics, Ringwood, Hampshire
Printed in Italy by A. Mondadori Editore, Verona

Contents

What is a mammal?

You are a mammal. Mammals are animals that are warm to touch because they have warm blood. Most mammals give birth to live babies – not eggs – and the mother produces milk for her babies to drink.

All mammals have some hair – even whales have a few.

As big as a house...
The biggest mammal of all is the blue whale, which is about the size of a house – a big house – and as heavy as 2,000 people!

...smaller than a mouse
The smallest mammal is the rare bumble-bee bat. With its wings outstretched it's only half the size of the blue whale's eye!

What a team!
There are thousands of different kinds of mammal. Some of them live in the water, but most of them live on land.

lion

sealion *hare* *zebra*

armadillo

You are a primate (pry-mate), one of a group of mammals that includes monkeys and gorillas. Some primates are very clever and learn quickly – thanks to their big, well-developed brains.

Slow starter

Human babies need their parents for far longer than any other mammal except the elephant. Humans can't walk or talk properly until they are one or two. Then they have to go to school to learn to read and write. By the time they've learned how to look after themselves properly, they're about 16 years old.

Shake those bones!

All mammals have a skeleton, a frame of bones inside their bodies. This skeleton is built around a backbone. Animals with backbones are called vertebrates (*ver-tuh-brayts*) because the little bones that make up the backbone are called vertebrae (*ver-tuh-bray*).

kangaroo

giraffe

wolf

peccary

beaver

9

The elephant

Elephants are big – very big. They are the largest land animals of all. A grown-up elephant is taller than a bus – and weighs as much as a van full of people!

six-year-old

newborn calf

Indian elephant

An elephant's tusks are just overgrown teeth.

Big ears
Elephants live in India and Africa. Indian elephants flap their big ears to keep cool in the hot jungles. But Africa can get even hotter, and an African elephant's ears are even bigger.

The most amazing part of an elephant is its trunk – which is really a very long, all-in-one nose and top lip.

Nose pipe
Elephants use their trunks for all kinds of things. They smell with it. They grasp food and touch each other with it. They squirt water into their mouths and shower their backs with it. They even use their trunks to trumpet loudly.

Women's club

Female elephants and their children stick close together in family herds. Everywhere they go, they are usually led by the biggest female, called the matriarch. Grown-up males spend most of their lives alone.

matriarch

teenage
male

The elephant's wisdom

Elephants are said to be very wise. In ancient Siam, people believed that if you whispered a problem in the ear of an elephant, the elephant would give a sign to tell you how to solve it.

The big toenail of an adult elephant is bigger than your whole hand.

Tree trunks

To eat, elephants tear off leaves and branches with their trunks or rip up bunches of grass. Sometimes they rip up whole trees, roots and all!

11

The camel

What a strange-looking beast! But nature has a reason for everything. The camel lives in deserts where there is little to eat or drink, and its body has adapted to go for a long time without food and water.

Where do I sit?
When riding a two-hump camel, you sit between the humps. On a one-hump camel you perch in a saddle on top of the hump.

Thirst – no problem!
A camel rarely gets thirsty. Its body uses so little water that it can go for 10 months without a drink! The camel shrivels to a bag of bones, but one big drink and it's back to normal.

Here's the problem!
Camels may be useful, but they can be bad-tempered and smelly.

Work – no problem!
Without camels, life for desert people would be hard. Camels carry heavy loads and provide milk to drink and good, thick wool to wear.

Heat – no problem!
A camel can really take the heat. Unlike us, it doesn't have much fat under its skin to keep in the heat.

A camel stores most of its fat in one place – its hump.

Sand – no problem!
The camel's feet are just the thing for the desert. Each one has two big toes that spread apart to stop the camel from sinking into the sand.

One hump or two?
Sturdy bactrian camels from the deserts of Asia have not one hump but two.

Dromedary
Most camels live in Arabia and Africa. They just have one hump and are called "dromedaries".

13

The fox

Foxes are part of the dog family. They sleep all day in their underground burrows and come out at night to search the woods and fields for food.

Secret stores
Foxes don't just hunt for food when they're hungry. Sometimes they hide food in a secret place in case they get hungry later.

The mouse leap
Mice are tricky to catch. The clever fox sneaks up softly. Then it jumps up high and dives down right on top of its prey.

Foxed!
Foxes are famous for their cunning. An old story tells how a fox tricks a crow into dropping a piece of cheese. The fox flatters the crow and asks it to sing. When the vain bird opens its beak, out pops the cheese.

A fox's ears are so sensitive it can hear a worm wriggling on the other side of a field.

Mmm, tasty!
Foxes eat just about anything, from worms to chickens. Some even sneak into town and raid dustbins.

Arctic fox
Not all foxes are red. One kind of fox lives in the Arctic, where its white winter coat is a perfect disguise in the snow.

Foxy sounds
Foxes yap, howl, bark, and whimper, just like dogs do.

Family life
A mother fox gives birth to around five little cubs at one time. She looks after them while the father fox goes out to search for food. Both the mother and the father teach their cubs to hunt and fight by playing games with them.

15

A flying fox?

With its furry snout and big eyes, this strange creature looks like a little fox. But it's not. It's a fruit-eating bat or "flying fox" and it can fly as well as a bird.

Fruit detector
Some Mexican fruit bats love ripe bananas – so much so that Mexican farmers have to harvest their crop before it ripens. But the bat's sharp nose can even smell out ripe bananas inside a farmer's hut!

Bat club
Most bats are creatures of the night. During the day, they hang upside-down in trees and caves, snoozing, chattering, and cleaning their wings. From a distance they look like closed umbrellas.

Juice extractor
A fruit bat has a mouth like a lemon squeezer. The bat uses its tongue to squash fruit against special horny ridges in the roof of its mouth. When all the juice is squeezed out, it spits out the skin and pips.

Flying foxes grab fruit without landing.

Going batty
The world is full of bats – nearly 1,000 different kinds altogether. This Egyptian fruit bat is just one of more than 170 different kinds of flying fox.

finger *finger*

arm

thumb

arm

leg

foot

tail

Flying fingers
A bat's wing is a thin, see-through layer of skin and muscle. This layer is stretched tight between the bat's bony legs, arms, tail, and great long fingers.

Earsight

Most bats eat insects, not fruit. These bats can chase their prey in the dark by using their ears. They make very high squeaks and listen to the way the squeaks bounce back from nearby objects.

Vampires

The evil Count Dracula – who sucks people's blood – has given vampire bats a bad name. Vampire bats do drink blood, but usually from cows and pigs, not humans. They do live in old castles, though.

The sloth

Sloths spend most of their lives hanging upside-down in trees in the rain forests of South America. They move very slowly and only wake up at night.

What is a sloth?
The word sloth means someone who is very, very lazy and slow – just like the sloth, in fact.

Too lazy to wash
Sloths don't clean their fur. After a while it grows a greenish scum and moths and beetles come to live in it. This is a good disguise – it makes the sloth look like a bunch of leaves.

What a drag!
Sloths' legs aren't made for walking. If they ever find themselves on the ground (which doesn't happen very often), they have to drag themselves along with their claws.

Going for a swim

They're not good at washing, they're not good at walking, but sloths are surprisingly good at swimming in the jungle rivers.

The sloth's claws are huge built-in hooks for hanging from branches.

The sloth's fur grows backwards so that water can drip off it.

Upside-down babies

Mother sloths even give birth to their babies hanging upside-down. The baby crawls into the fur on its mother's tummy and searches for a nipple. It stays there for up to nine months, drinking milk until it is ready to start hanging upside-down all by itself.

The otter

Otters are more at home in the water than on land. Most of them live in rivers and streams, and one kind spends its whole life in the sea. All otters are good swimmers with long, slender bodies and strong tails.

Otter nonsense
They are very playful animals. When otters are not hunting, they spend hours play-fighting, diving, and sliding down muddy banks into the river.

Funny feet
The back feet of an otter are webbed and look just like flippers.

Sweet dreams
Sea otters even sleep in the water, lying on their backs. The otter wraps itself in seaweed so it won't be swept away while it's snoozing.

Warm fur
This is a river otter from Asia. Like all otters it has lovely, soft, silky fur. The fur traps bubbles of air to keep the otter warm.

On your marks, get set...
Otters are fast and graceful swimmers. A sea otter can swim at 16 km/h – that's faster than you can run.

Laying the table
The sea otter eats floating on its back. It uses its chest as a table, and often balances a flat stone like a plate on its chest. The otter then smashes clams and crabs on the stone to open them.

Unlike most water animals, the otter doesn't have a layer of fat under its skin for warmth.

Big appetites
Otters eat a lot of food, mainly fish and shell-fish. They use their long whiskers to find their food on the bottom of the river or sea. If an otter catches a really big fish, it may hold the fish to its chest with its front feet, then take it to the bank to munch at its leisure.

The squirrel monkey

This pretty little monkey lives in big groups in the jungles of South America. As many as 500 monkeys may travel together through the treetops, leaping from branch to branch like acrobats in the circus.

All dressed up

Squirrel monkeys have always been popular as pets. It was once fashionable to have hats and coats made for pet monkeys. Then people would walk down the street with their pet sitting on one shoulder.

The monkey uses its long tail for balance as it walks along branches.

All fingers and thumbs

The squirrel monkey uses its hands like hooks to catch on to branches. It has long, strong fingers. But its thumbs are so far up its wrists it can't use them for grasping the way we can.

For its size, the squirrel monkey has the biggest brain of any animal – including you!

Drinking and dozing
Baby monkeys cling to their mother's fur and ride around on her back. They spend the first weeks of their lives drinking milk and sleeping, just like human babies.

Monkey menu
Squirrel monkeys live on leaves, fruit, and birds' eggs, spiced with insects and spiders and the occasional bunch of flowers.

Fur wash
Squirrel monkeys are very finicky when it comes to personal hygiene. They are always licking and brushing their fur. The monkey cleans its legs, stomach, and tail with its fingers, and uses its toes to comb its back, head, and behind its ears.

The porcupine

This spiky-looking creature is really a kind of overgrown guinea pig. It has sharp spines, or quills, and amazingly long whiskers.

Prickly babies
Baby porcupines are born with bristles that harden into sharp quills within a few hours.

Gripping tails
Unlike their African cousins, these American porcupines spend a lot of time in the treetops. They grip the branches using their long tails and strong claws.

Good manners
Porcupines are neat eaters. They hold their food against the ground with their front paws and chomp into it with their big, sharp teeth.

gnawing teeth

skull

Long in the tooth
The porcupine is a rodent. This means it has long, sharp front teeth for gnawing. As quickly as the teeth wear down they grow again. In fact, they never stop growing!

This African porcupine uses its whiskers to find its way in dark burrows.

Ouch!

Porcupine quills come loose and will stay stuck in the skin of an enemy. If germs get into the wound, even an animal as big as a lion may die.

Shake, rattle, and stab

When in danger, a porcupine will turn its back on its attacker, rattle its quills, grunt, and stamp its feet. If all this bluffing doesn't work, it reverses into its enemy, quills first.

A porcupine will rattle the hollow quills on its tail to scare off an attacker.

Punky hairdo

The porcupine's quills are specially adapted hairs that stand up without hairspray!

The tiger

Tigers are the largest of the big cats. This little cub is only ten weeks old but when it grows up it will be a powerful hunter. At one time tigers nearly died out, as thousands were killed for their beautiful skins. Today all tigers are protected by law.

In for the kill

A tiger begins searching for its prey by sniffing the air. Once it can see its victim, the tiger creeps up stealthily until it's near enough to charge. It attacks from the side or behind, slashing with its paws and then killing with a quick bite to the throat.

Do tigers eat people?

Generally, no. But if a tiger is old or sick and too slow to catch its usual prey, it may start attacking people.

Blind and toothless

Like kittens, tiger cubs are born blind and without teeth. Their stripes are lightly coloured and will get darker and darker as they grow.

Tiger tots

While the mother tiger looks after her cubs on her own, the father tiger prowls his range, warning other tigers to keep away.

In black and white

White tigers are rarely found in the wild but are quite common in zoos.

Water sports

Tigers are strong swimmers. If a tiger cannot find enough large animals to eat, it will head for a river and snatch fish and even frogs from the water.

Like all cats, a tiger can pull in its claws – until it needs them for catching its prey.

Hide and seek

The stripes on the tiger's coat blend in with the sunshine and shadows of the forest. It can sneak up on its prey quietly without being seen.

Bringing up baby

Baby mammals start to grow inside their mothers and stay in there until they are ready to be born. Then their parents look after them until they are old enough to look after themselves.

A bear that's not a bear
The koala is a very cuddly little animal. It looks like a bear, but isn't a bear at all. It's really a marsupial (*mar-soo-pee-al*), a sort of mammal that carries its babies in a pouch on its belly. Like many other marsupials, the koala is only found in the wild in Australia.

Hanging out with mum
When a koala baby is born, it's hardly developed at all. It is pink and wrinkly and as small as a pea. The baby crawls into its mother's cosy pouch, latches on to a nipple, and doesn't let go for five months. It grows quietly, drinking milk and sleeping. When it's big enough, the baby koala starts to hop in and out of the pouch.

Mother giraffe with calf

Mother's milk
Mammals like the platypus and the koala are strange cases. Most mammals give birth to live babies which don't need a pouch. The first thing they do, other than cry, is look for a nipple and have a good drink of milk.

A mammal that lays eggs
The platypus looks like a small otter with a duck's bill for a nose. It's actually a bizarre sort of mammal that lays eggs. Platypuses are very primitive. They may have been around 70 million years ago, when the dinosaurs still walked the Earth.

A pregnant elephant has to wait 22 months before her baby is born. That's almost two years – longer than any other mammal.

	Usual number of babies	Time baby is inside mother	Age baby stops drinking mother's milk	
Human being	1	9 months	6-9 months	
African elephant	1	22 months	3-4 years	
Dromedary camel	1	14 months	9-18 months	
Red fox	4-6	7 weeks	8-10 weeks	
Egyptian fruit bat	1	4 months	3-5 months	
Linne's two-toed sloth	1	6 months	3-4 weeks	
Asian short-clawed otter	3	2 months	3-4 months	
Black-capped squirrel monkey	1	5 months	5-6 months	
African porcupine	1-3	4 months	4-6 weeks	
Indian tiger	3-4	15 weeks	3-5 months	
Koala	1-2	7 weeks	6-12 months	